MAKING THE GRADE · GRADE 4

EASY POPULAR PIECES FOR YOUNG PIANISTS. SELECTED AND ARRANGED BY LYNDA FRITH

Exclusive distributors:
Music Sales Limited
Newmarket Road, Bury St. Edmunds, Suffolk IP33 3YB.
This book © Copyright 1995 Chester Music
ISBN 0-7119-5052-0
Order No. CH61084
Cover design and typesetting by Pemberton & Whiteoord.
Printed in the United Kingdom by
Caligraving Limited, Thetford, Norfolk.

Unauthorised reproduction of any part of this publication by any means
including photocopying is an infringement of copyright.

Chester Music

(A division of Music Sales Limited)
14/15 Berners Street, London W1T 3LJ.

INTRODUCTION

This collection of 12 popular tunes has been carefully arranged and graded to provide attractive teaching repertoire for young pianists. New concepts and techniques are introduced progressively, and the familiarity of the material will stimulate pupils' enthusiasm and encourage their practice. The standard of the pieces progresses to Associated Board Grade 4.

CONTENTS

DON'T CRY FOR ME ARGENTINA

by Andrew Lloyd Webber & Tim Rice

Legato pedalling will enhance the mood of this piece. Be careful to play the left hand quavers quietly and evenly.

At bar 27 the right hand still plays the tune, but in the tenor register, while the left hand crosses over.

© Copyright 1976, 1977 for the World by Evita Music Limited, London W6.
All Rights Reserved. International Copyright Secured.

I DREAMED A DREAM

by Claude-Michel Schonberg & Herbert Kretzmer

Try to make the descending minims in the left hand as legato as possible. The fingering shown will help you to achieve this.

© Copyright (Music & Lyrics) 1980 Editions Musicales Alain Boublil
English lyrics © Copyright 1985 Alain Boublil Music Limited. This arrangement © Copyright 1995 Alain Boublil Music Limited.
All Rights Reserved. International Copyright Secured.

MORE THAN WORDS

by Nuno Bettencourt & Gary Cherone

The syncopation in this piece creates some difficult rhythms.
Practise slowly, counting aloud, or use a metronome to keep in time.

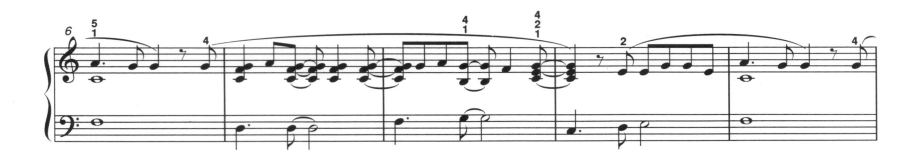

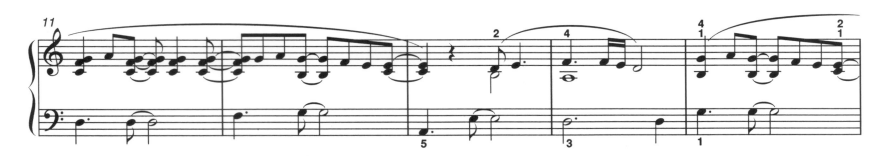

© Copyright 1990 Almo Music Corporation/Funky Metal Publishing, USA. Rights administered for
the UK, Eire & PRS Territories (except Hong Kong, Malaysia & Singapore) by Rondor Music (London) Limited,
10a Parsons Green, London SW6 4TW. All Rights Reserved. International Copyright Secured.

DON'T KNOW MUCH

by Barry Mann, Tom Snow & Cynthia Weil

The right hand plays the tune (shown by the slurs).

It also plays some of the accompaniment notes, and these should be softer so that the tune stands out clearly.

© Copyright 1980 ATV Music Corporation, Mann & Weil Songs Incorporated & Braintree Music, USA/Snow Music, USA. ATV Music, London WC2.
All Rights Reserved. International Copyright Secured.

TEARS IN HEAVEN

by Eric Clapton & Will Jennings

Bars 19 to 26 contain plenty of chords. Practise carefully to create as legato a sound as possible, but be aware of the phrasing.

© Copyright 1991 & 1995 E.C. Music Limited, London NW1 (87.5%).
© Copyright 1991 Blue Sky Rider Songs administered by Rondor Music (London) Limited, 10a Parsons Green, London SW6 for the World (excluding USA & Canada) (12.5%).
All Rights Reserved. International Copyright Secured.

OH, PRETTY WOMAN

by Roy Orbison & Bill Dees

The left hand phrase in bar one occurs frequently.
Make an exercise of it to establish it firmly under the fingers.

© Copyright 1964 renewed 1992 Orbi-Lee Music, R-Key Darkus Music & Acuff-Rose Music Incorporated, USA.
Acuff-Rose Music Limited, London W1.
All Rights Reserved. International Copyright Secured.

16

CLAIR DE LUNE

by Claude Debussy

Experiment with the sustaining pedal. The piece requires a veiled, atmospheric sound, especially in bars 15 to 18.

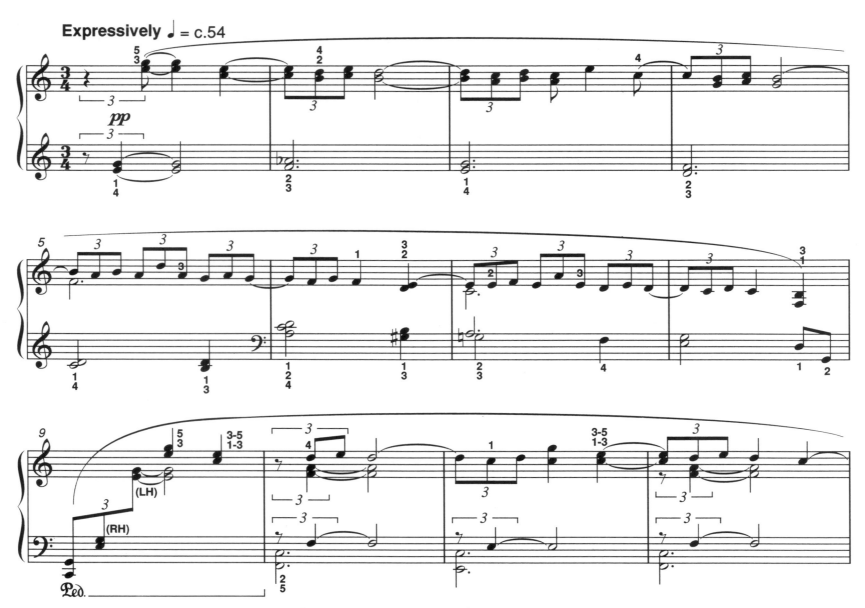

© Copyright 1995 Chester Music Limited, 8/9 Frith Street, London W1.
All Rights Reserved. International Copyright Secured.

19

TAKE FIVE

by Paul Desmond

Practise the first right hand phrase carefully, paying particular attention to the fingering. Practise *slowly* at first.

© Copyright 1960 and 1961 by Derry Music Company, USA. Controlled by Valentine Music Group Limited for the World
(excluding USA, Canada, Japan, Germany, Austria, Australasia, Scandinavia, Finland, Iceland, France, Benelux, Italy, Republic of South Africa and Rhodesia).
All Rights Reserved. International Copyright Secured.

21

COULD IT BE MAGIC?

by Barry Manilow & Adrienne Anderson

Make sure you sustain all the semibreves in the last nine bars for their full value.
Chopin's 'Prelude in C Minor' is quoted at the beginning and end of this piece.

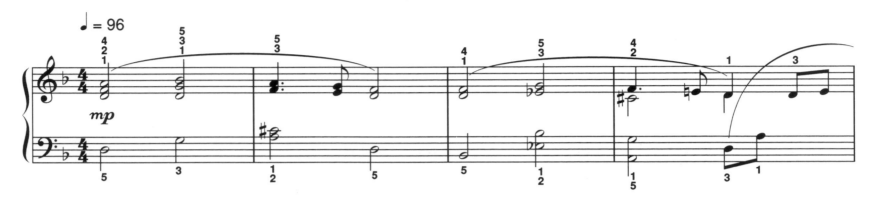

© Copyright 1973 Careers-BMG Music Publishing Incorporated/Angela Music/Open Curtain Publishing, USA.
BMG Music Publishing Limited, 69-79 Fulham High Street, London SW6. This arrangement © 1995 BMG Music Publishing Limited.
All Rights Reserved. International Copyright Secured.

23

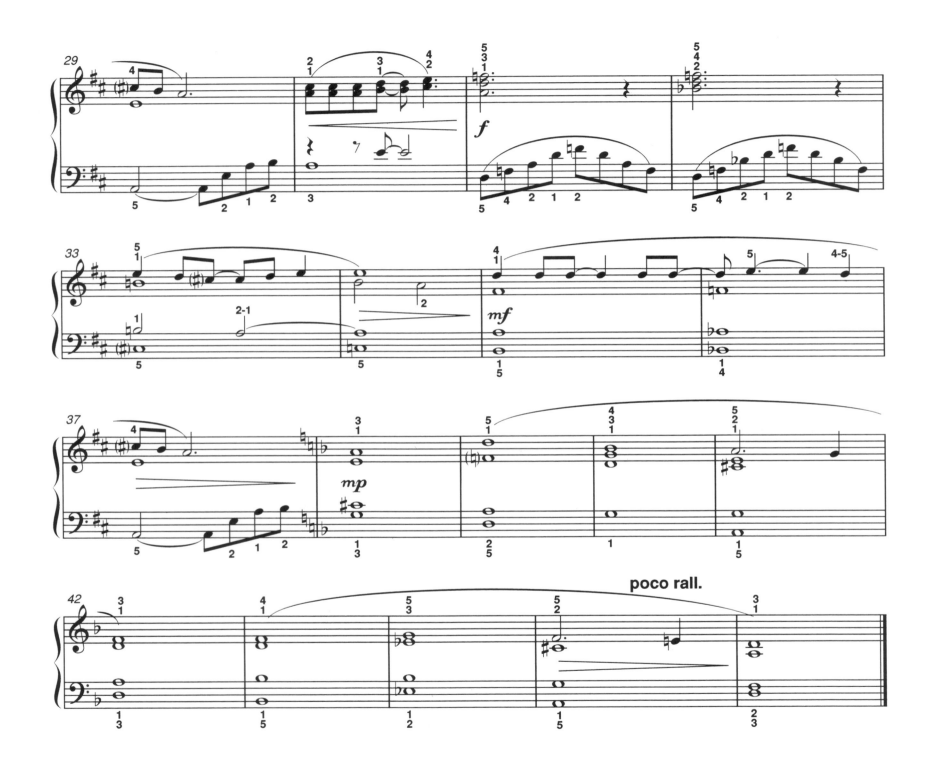

GOLLIWOGG'S CAKEWALK

by Claude Debussy

Pay attention to the dynamics and marks of expression to bring out the character of the music. Keep a very steady tempo.

© Copyright 1995 Chester Music Limited, 8/9 Frith Street, London W1.
All Rights Reserved. International Copyright Secured.

STRAWBERRY FIELDS FOREVER

by John Lennon & Paul McCartney

This piece has some interesting rhythms in it. Practise bars 9 to 12 in particular, counting carefully.

© Copyright 1967 Northern Songs.
All Rights Reserved. International Copyright Secured.

THE SWAN

by Camille Saint-Saëns

The left hand needs to be played as smoothly as possible, allowing the right hand tune to sing out.

© Copyright 1995 Chester Music Limited, 8/9 Frith Street, London W1.
All Rights Reserved. International Copyright Secured.

23456789